I Remember Not Sleeping

Poetry by Sherri Levine
Illustrations by Moises Camacho

More information about the author and the book at:
www.sherrilevine.com

Copyright © 2024 Fernwood Press (*www.fernwoodpress.com*)

Illustrations by Moises Camacho (*www.mcartsgallery.com*)

Book design by Sam Rose Preminger (*www.sampreminger.com*)

ISBN: 978-1-59498-139-5

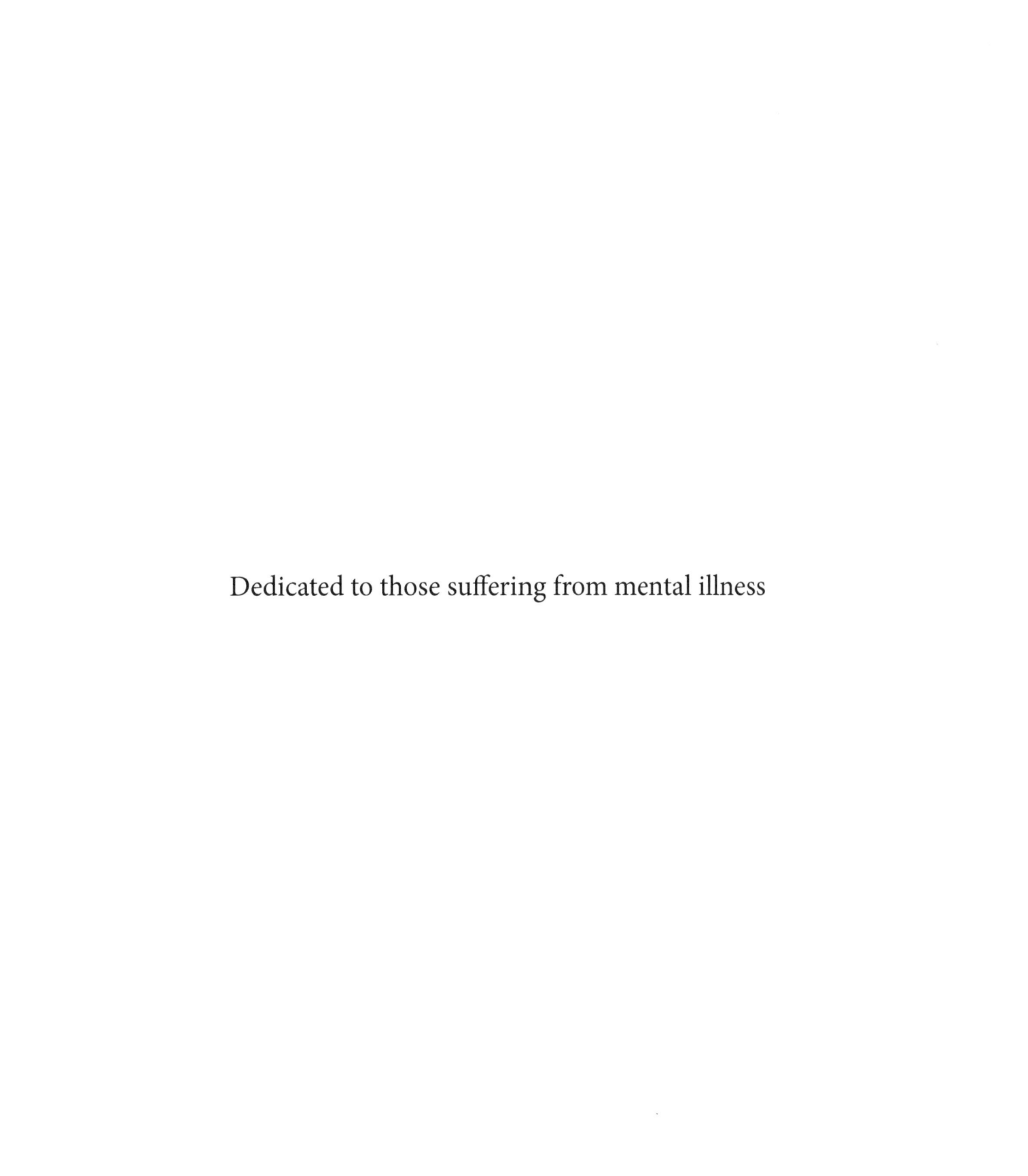

Dedicated to those suffering from mental illness

Praise for *I Remember Not Sleeping*

Each line, each page is a separate pathway into Sherri Levine's *I Remember Not Sleeping*. Some are straight or with curves you can't see beyond, and some are for just listening for the particular sound of the particular footstep. Accompanied by beautiful illustrations by Moises Camacho, Levine's poem intrigues and pulls the reader into a strange and fragile state of mind.

—Jason Renaud
Director, Mental Health Association of Portland

I am thrilled to recommend Sherri Levine's new collection of poetry. Through raw emotion and masterful use of language, she transforms private struggles into art that will resonate with readers. Sherri's passionate devotion to her craft is inspiring. I know readers will find solace, empowerment, and joy in these poems. It has been a gift to know Sherri and witness her talents over the years. Discover her work—it will stay with you.

—Kevin Fitts
Executive Director, Oregon Mental Health Consumers Association

In Sherri Levine's *I Remember Not Sleeping,* time and space collapses like a star. You can hear the poet receiving transmissions from Joe Brainard, from the gray walls of an institution, from her own soul, and in straightforward, lyric verse transmitting what she hears onto us. This poem is good company for anyone who has struggled with mental health, for anyone who has felt alone, for anyone being bounced around in the sea of life. Which is to say, it's a poem for all of us.

—Matthew Dickman
Author of *Husbandry*

In Sherri Levine's remarkable book, she uses words and images to illuminate the mystery, the pain, the desperate loneliness involved in mental illness. The artwork paired with almost every stanza moves the viewer and compels an emotional reaction. A tour de force.

—Pattie Palmer-Baker
Portland artist and poet

Foreword

1990

"I am not Sylvia Plath," I told the professor who sat across from me. His wire-framed, circular glasses slid down his long nose. "Tell us what the hospital is like," he said. I didn't want to do that. My visit with him was the only chance I got to leave the hospital. I am not Sylvia Plath. I am here. I am alive.

2023

I am blessed to have a partner, family, friends, and a psychiatrist who have supported and loved me to mental health. I feel grateful that I have been able to write and teach creative writing, encouraging others to share their work with the world. I am honored to share this book with you.

—Sherri Levine

I come to ferry you hence across the tide
To endless night, fierce fires and shramming cold.

–Dante
The Divine Comedy

Instead, a metal chair unfolds into a stretcher.
I lied secured there, but for my skipping mind.
They keep bustling.
Where you are going, Professor,
you won't need your Dante.

–Robert Lowell
"Visitors"

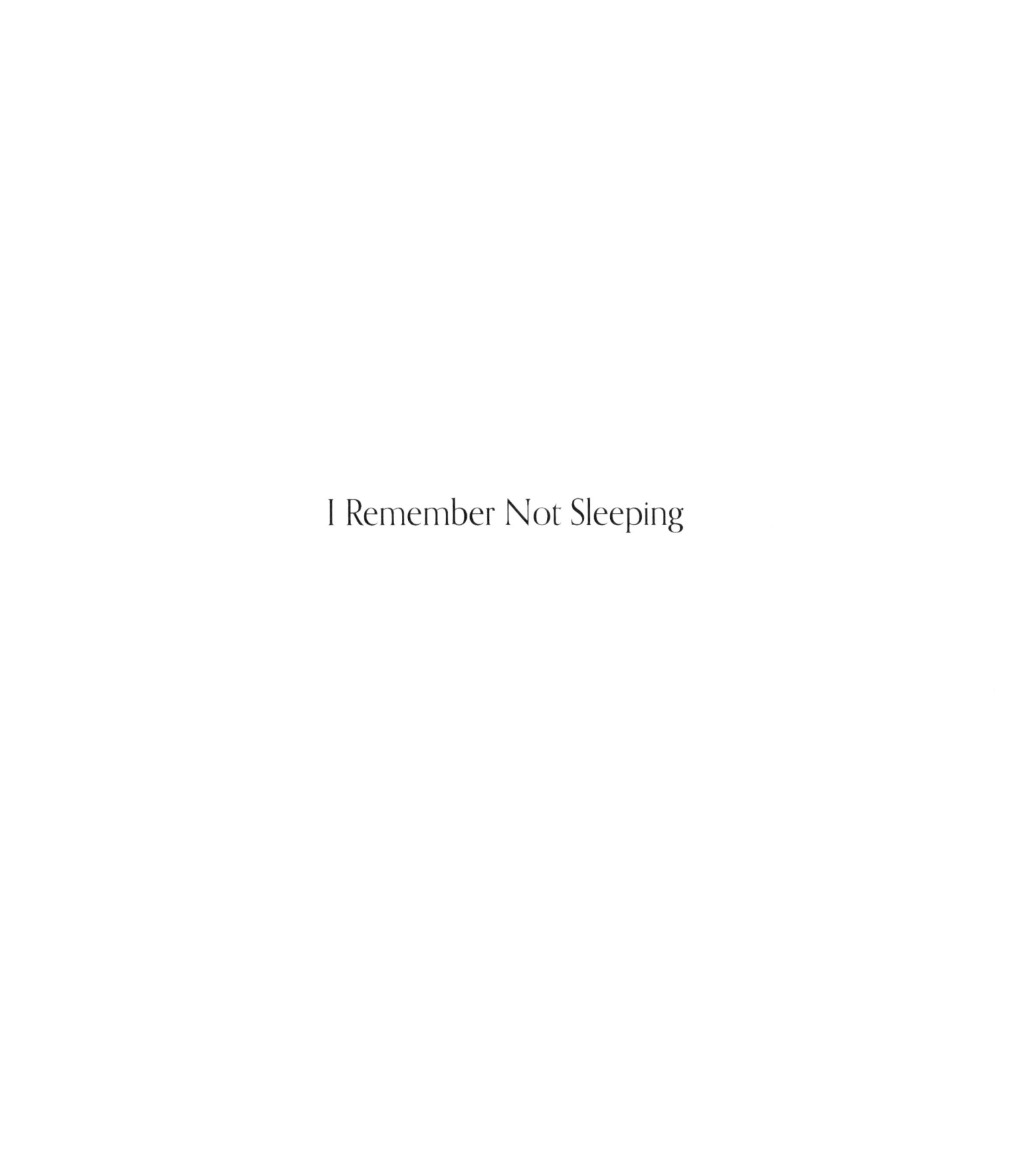

I Remember Not Sleeping

I remember lying on a squeaky cot in a room full of Czech women, listening to them breathe like lung machines.

I remember steam hissing from radiators, heels clicking down halls.

I remember, on the psychiatric ward, thinking that the patients were doctors who were there to save me because I was dying.

A flashlight shone in my eyes every two hours during the night, a needle poked my arm.

Someone always watched me in the shower with a flashlight.

I think I'll go turn myself off and go on down.
All the way down.
−Jimi Hendrix
"Manic Depression"

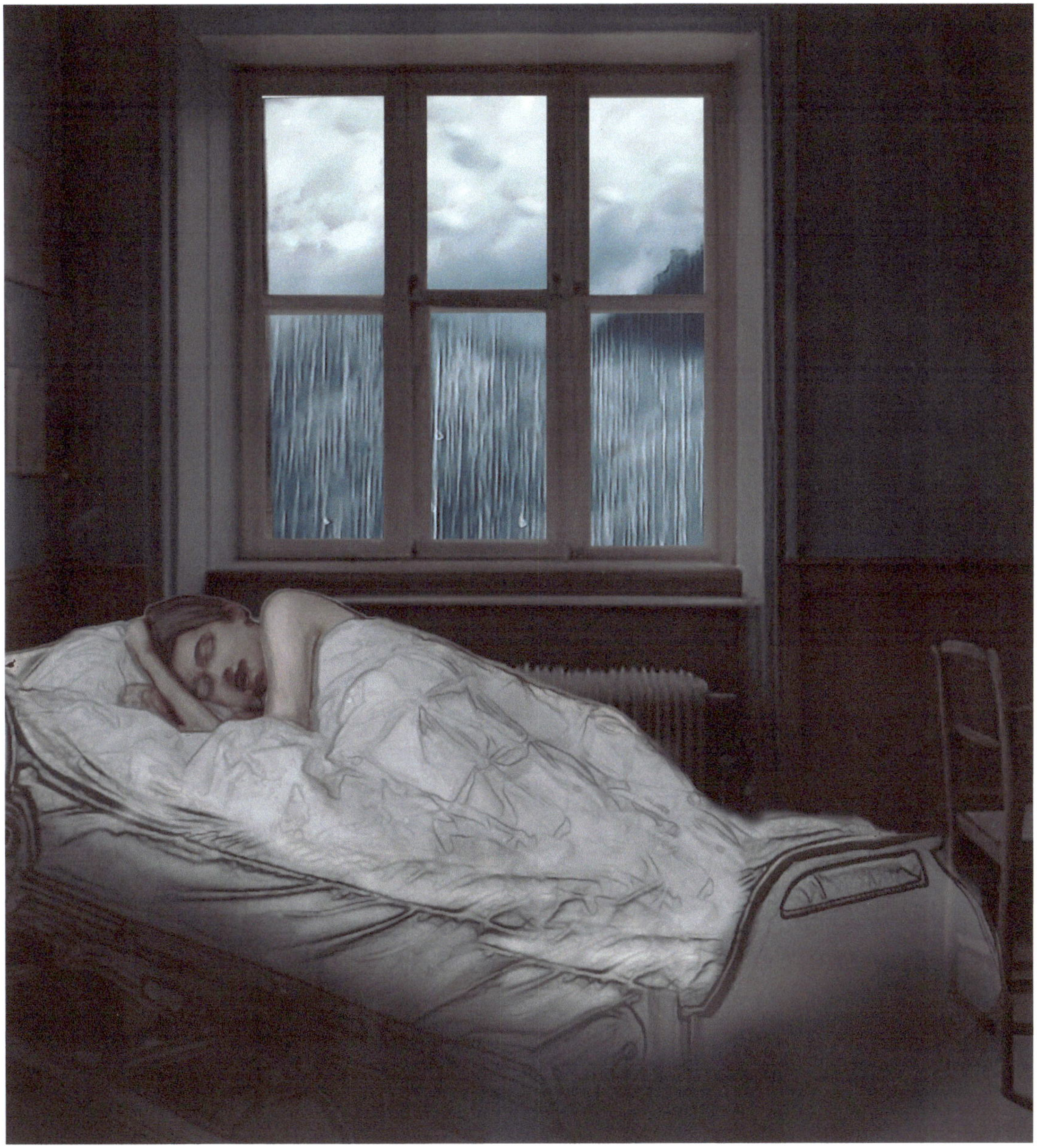

I remember waking up at night to use the bathroom and seeing Czech nurses watching porn on TV.

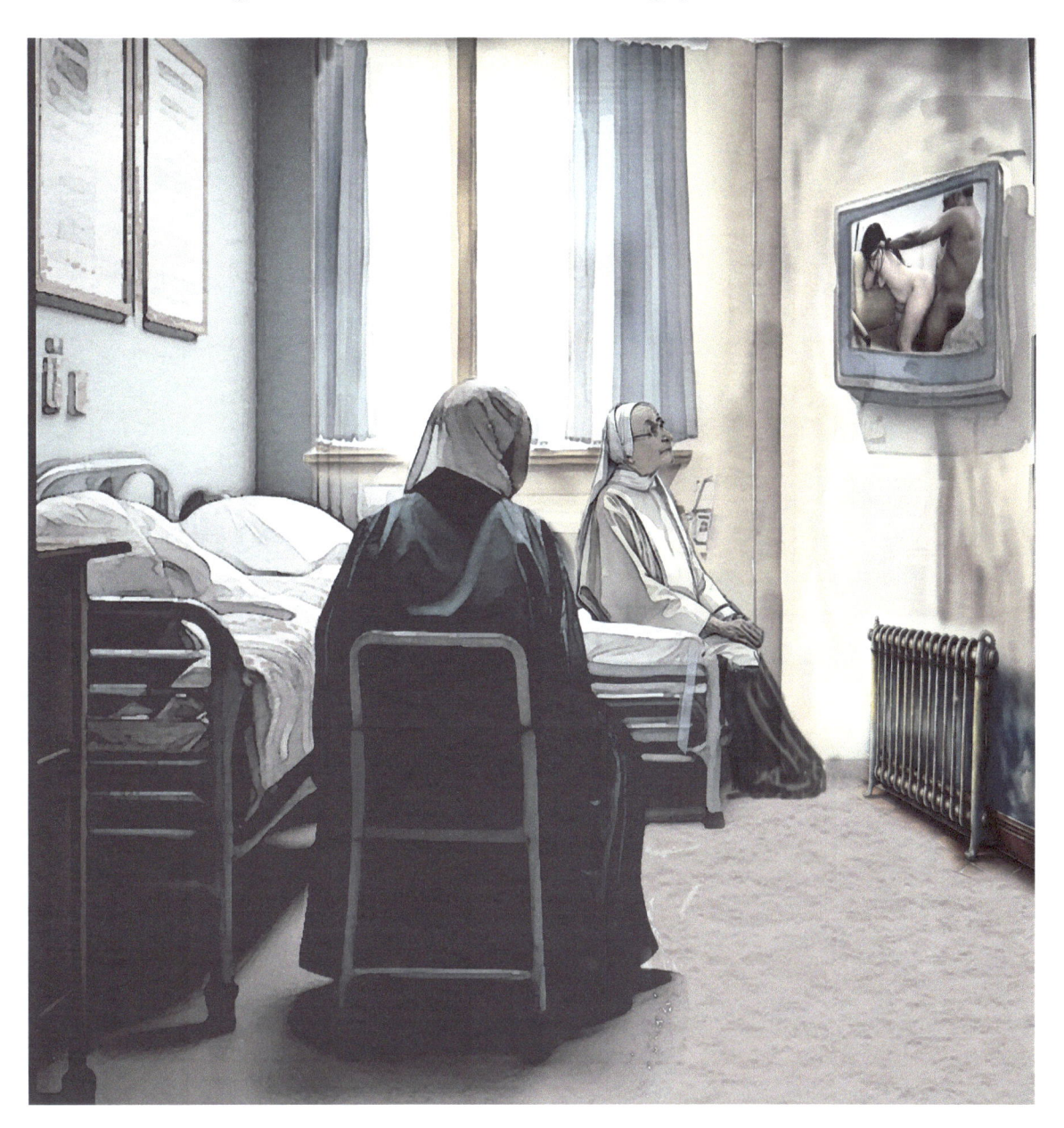

I remember having sex with men, multiple men, and women, but I don't remember feeling anything except sore.

I was never tired. And never hungry.

I got a day pass from the hospital and snuck into a man's car.

We smoked unfiltered Camels and listened to Metallica.

I hated heavy metal, but it felt good to be held.

*I have myself an inner weight of woe
That God himself can scarcely bear.*

–Theodore Roethke
"Elegy"

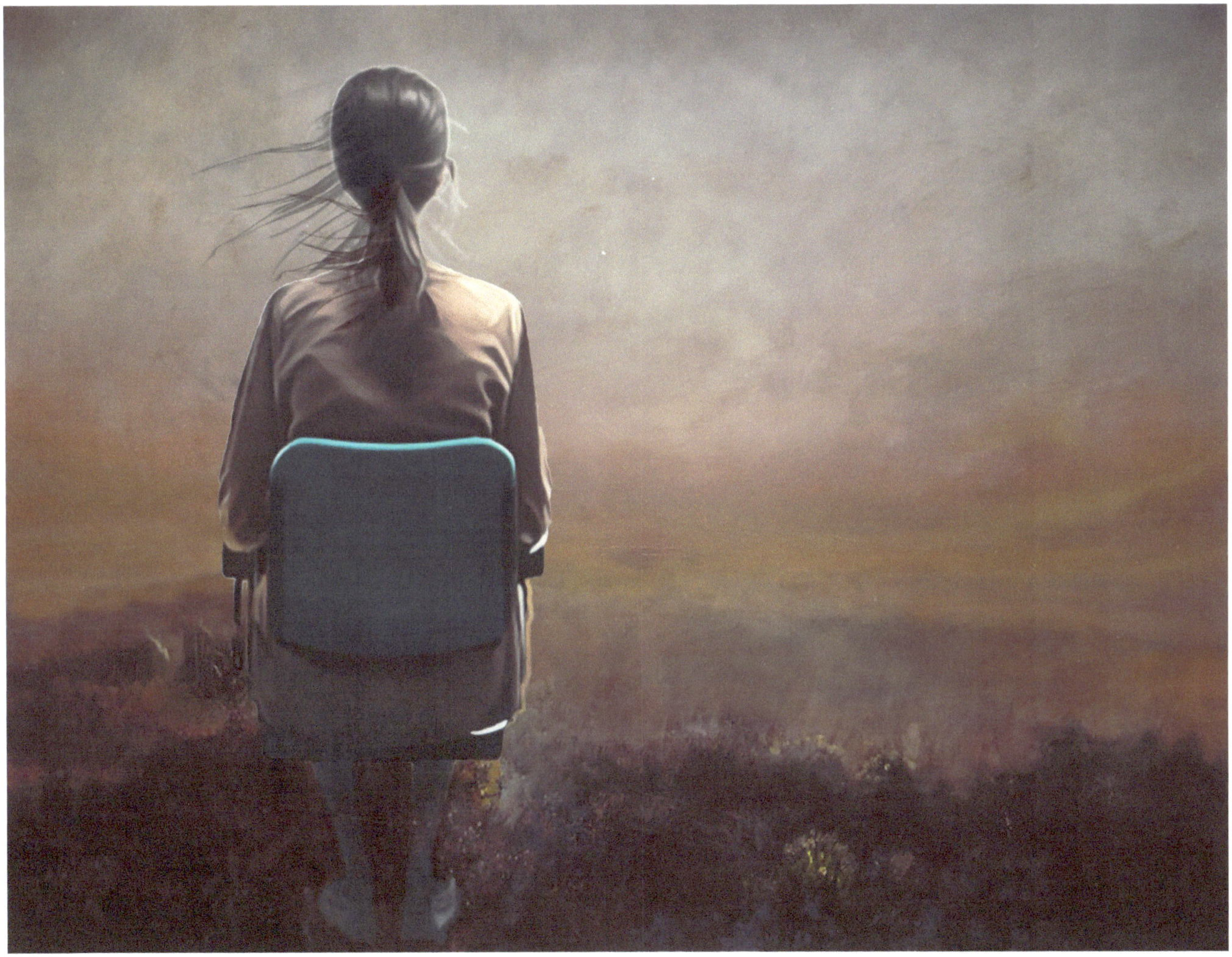

I remember the doctor asking me if I had been breastfed and what it meant to throw stones in glass houses.

I was afraid if I didn't
get the answers right,

something bad
would happen to me.

One doctor said sleep deprivation causes mania.

My roommate swallowed a crushed lightbulb.

I remember the bitter taste of pills I hid under my tongue.

I remember how good it was to come home—to stretch my legs across my bed, wrap myself in clean cotton sheets, and listen to the rain.

*To be reborn, again and again and again,
to be transformed all over again.*

–Delmore Schwartz
"May's Truth and May's Falsehood"

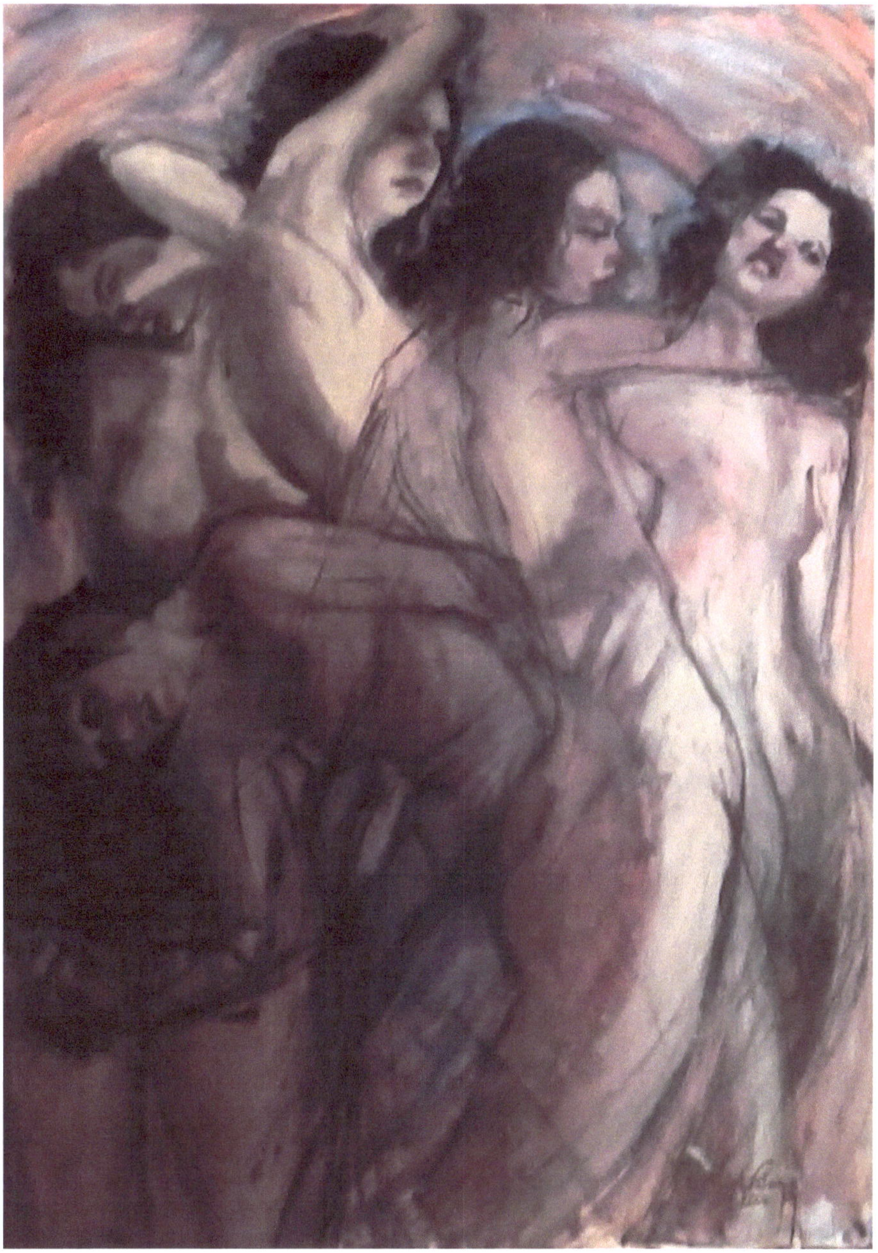

Snow fell on the last night in Prague
before I got on a plane to the States.

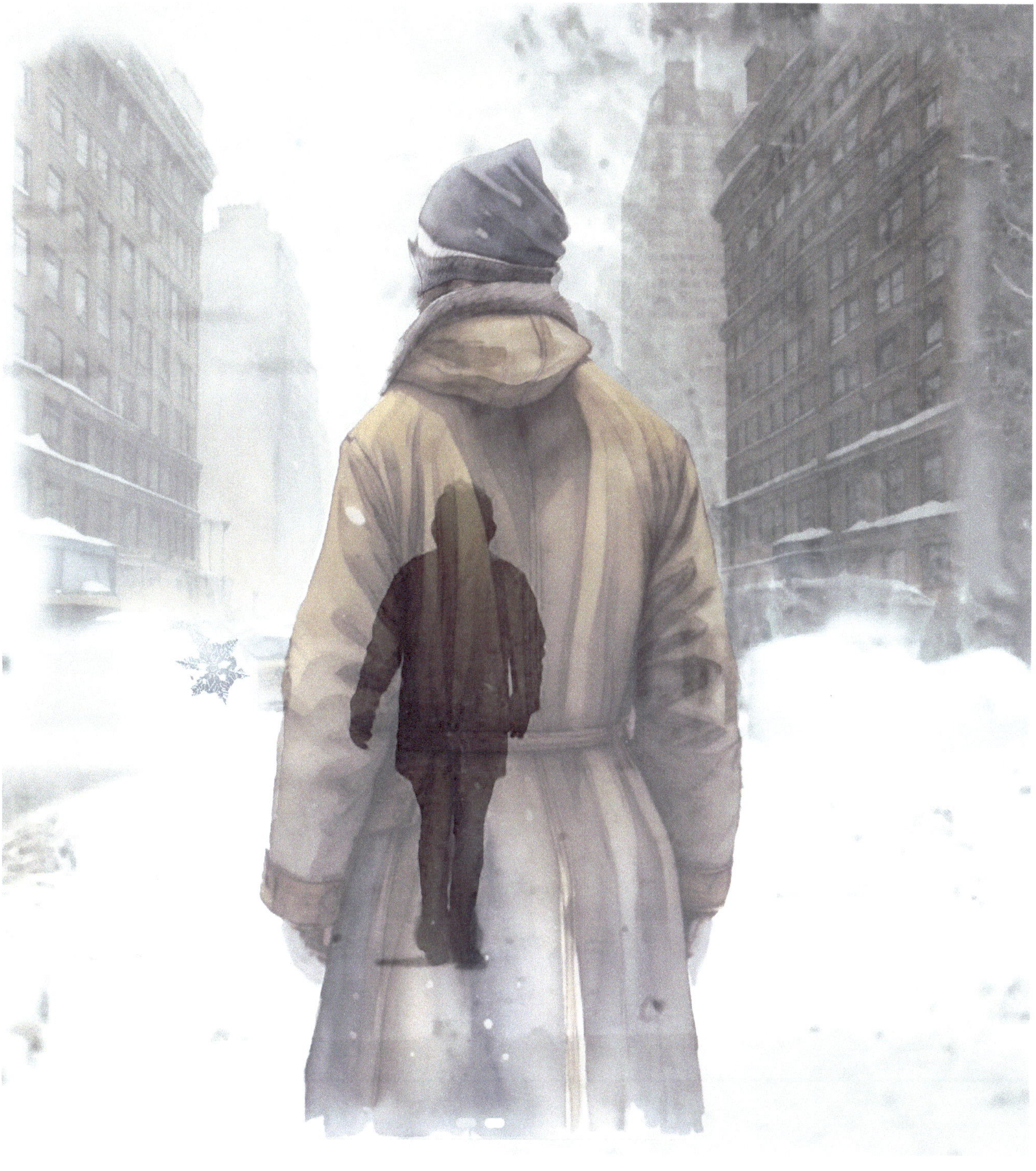

I wasn't sure I would come back, but I wasn't thinking about that.

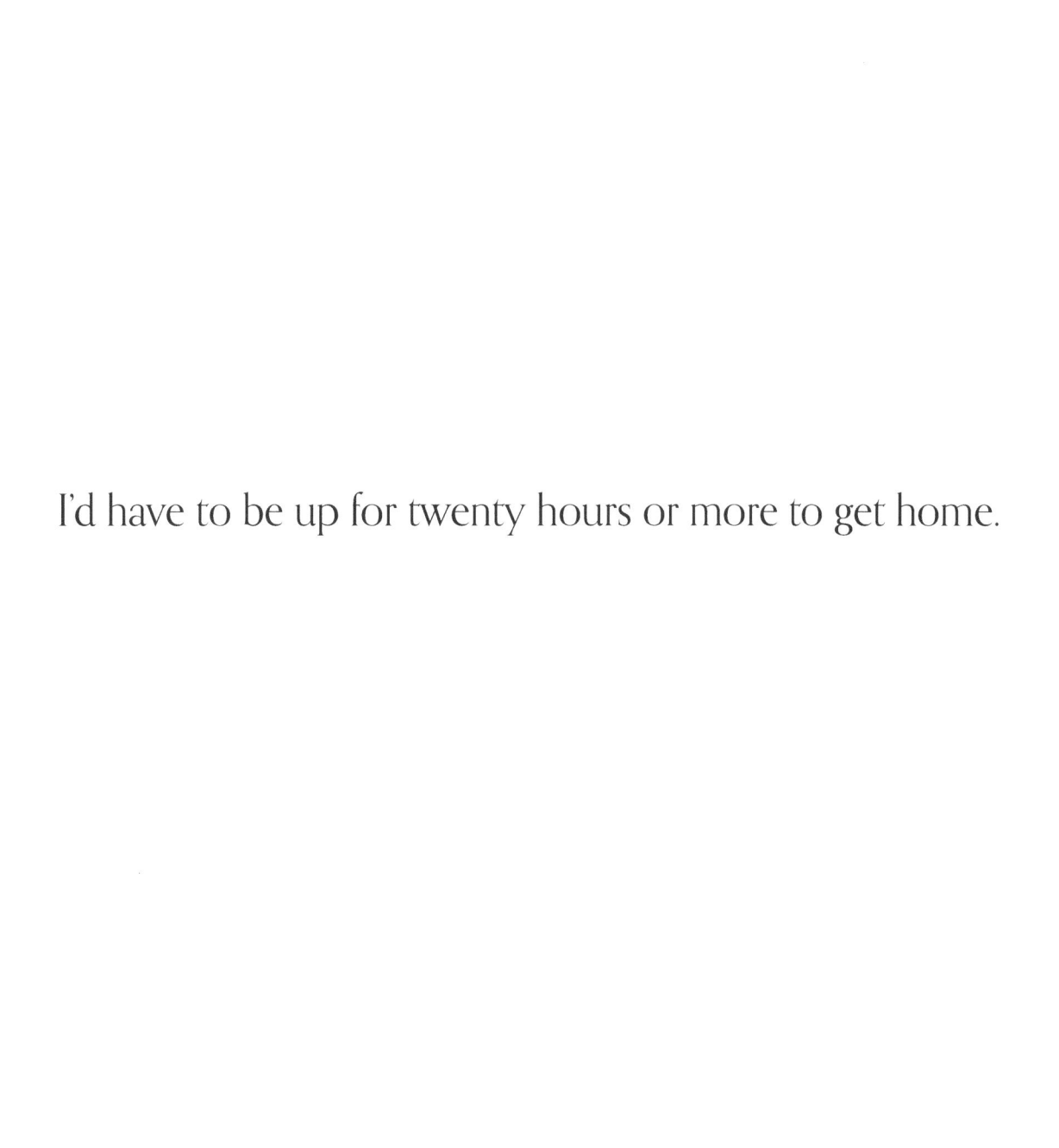

I'd have to be up for twenty hours or more to get home.

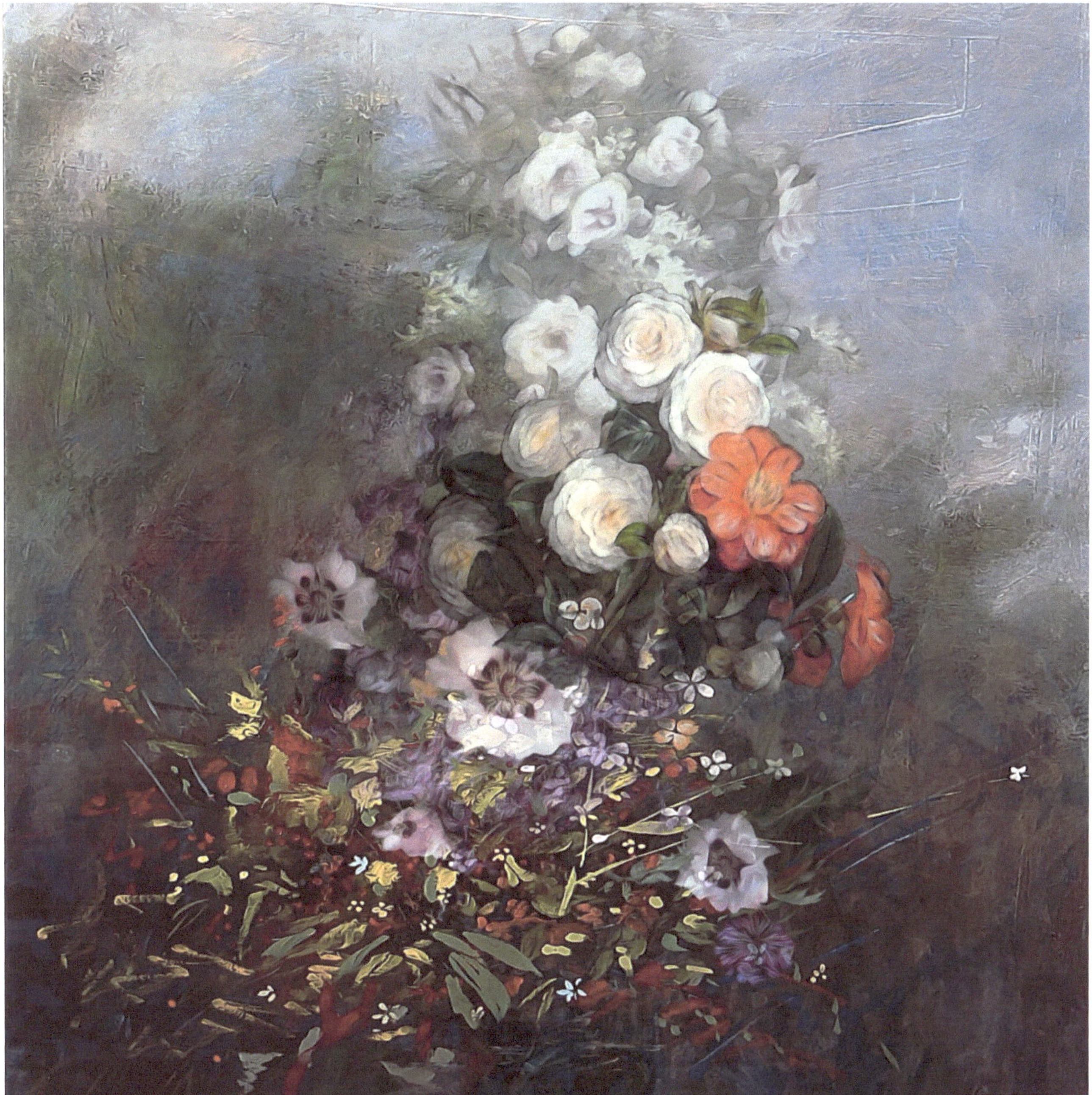

Acknowledgments

My deepest gratitude goes to

      Fernwood Press

      Sam Rose Preminger, editor and friend

      Joe Brainard, author of *I Remember*

      Ann Farley, proofreader and friend

      Dr. George Drinka

      Bob Lagattuta

This poem appeared in *Driftwood Press*, volume 6.2

The artwork on page forty-nine of this book is a photograph provided by the author, original artist unknown

Sherri Levine is an artist and poet living in Portland, Oregon. She won the Lois Cranston Memorial Award and first place in the Oregon Poetry Association contest. Her poems have been published in local and national journals such as *Prairie Schooner*, *Calyx*, *Poet Lore*, and *Jewish Literary Journal*. Her published books are a *Joy to See* (Just a Lark Books, 2024), *Stealing Flowers from the Neighbors* (Kelsay Press, 2021), and *In These Voices* (Poetry Box, 2018). She created Head for the Hills, a monthly poetry series. Originally from upstate New York, she escaped the harsh winters and is now soaking in the Oregon rain.

She can be found at sherrilevine.com

Moises Camacho was born in Mexico City and has lived in California since 2000. His traditional training allows him to create illustrations with classic media, watercolor, acrylic, and oil. Since 2009 he has directed the Orange County Fine Art Studio where he creates large format visual projects and murals in the city of Santa Ana, California, where there are more than seventeen public projects.

He can be found at mcartsgallery.com